FAVORITE FOOTBALL TEAMS

PITTSBURGH STEELERS

BY K. C. KELLEY

THE CHILD'S WORLD®

1980 Lookout Drive • Mankato, MN 56003-1705

800-599-READ • www.childsworld.com

ACKNOWLEDGMENTS

The Child's World®: Mary Berendes, Publishing Director

Shoreline Publishing Group, LLC: James Buckley, Jr., Production Director

The Design Lab: Kathleen Petelinsek, Design;

 Gregory Lindholm, Page Production

PHOTOS

Cover: Focus on Football

Interior: AP/Wide World: 9, 18; Focus on Football: 5, 7, 10, 13, 17, 21, 22, 23,

 25, 27; Stockexpert: 14

LIBRARY OF CONGRESS

CATALOGING-IN-PUBLICATION DATA

Kelley, K. C.

 Pittsburgh Steelers / by K.C. Kelley.

 p. cm. — (Favorite football teams)

 Includes bibliographical references and index.

 ISBN 978-1-60253-319-6 (library bound : alk. paper)

 1. Pittsburgh Steelers (Football team)—History—Juvenile literature.

I. Title. II. Series.

 GV956.P57K45 2009

 796.332'640974886—dc22   2009009069

Published in the United States of America

Mankato, Minnesota

March, 2010

PA02047

TABLE OF CONTENTS

Go, Steelers!

Steel is hard. The Steelers might just be harder! The Pittsburgh Steelers are one of football's oldest and toughest teams. They didn't play very well for a long, long time. But in the 1970s they became one of the best teams around. In recent years, they've been among the best again. Let's meet the mighty Steelers!

Here come the Steelers! Anthony Madison (37) leads the team as they run onto the field for a game in 2008.

Who Are the Pittsburgh Steelers?

The Pittsburgh Steelers play in the National Football League (NFL). They are one of 32 teams in the NFL. The NFL includes the National Football Conference (NFC) and the American Football Conference (AFC). The Steelers play in the North Division of the AFC. The winner of the NFC plays the winner of the AFC in the **Super Bowl**. The Steelers have been the NFL champions six times!

A trio of Steelers crashes through the line. They are trying to block this kick by the Dallas Cowboys.

Where They Came From

The Steelers began in 1933 as the Pittsburgh Pirates. A man named Art Rooney paid the NFL $2,500 to let him start this new team. He chose the name to copy the baseball team. In 1940, the team changed its name to the Steelers. Why Steelers? Factories around Pittsburgh make a lot of steel! For a long time, the Steelers didn't win many games. They didn't even win a playoff game until 1972!

Quarterback **Terry Bradshaw (12)** and running back **Franco Harris (32)** were part of the first great Pittsburgh Steelers teams in the 1970s.

Who They Play

The Steelers play 16 games each season. There are three other teams in the AFC North. They are the Baltimore Ravens, the Cincinnati Bengals, and the Cleveland Browns. Every year, the Steelers play each of these teams twice. They also play other teams in the AFC and NFC. The Steelers and the Ravens are big **rivals**. Both teams love to play **defense**. Their games are known for hard hitting and low scores.

"Big Ben" Roethlisberger gets set to make a pass. He and the Steelers are battling the Bengals, another AFC North team.

Where They Play

The Steelers play their home games at Heinz Field. This stadium opened in 2001. It's a great place to watch football! A food company paid the Steelers to name the stadium. The Steelers used to play in Three Rivers Stadium. That stadium got its name for the three rivers that meet in Pittsburgh.

Don't worry, this picture isn't fuzzy. Those white blobs are snowflakes! Fans and players have to deal with winter weather at Heinz Field in Pittsburgh.

84 LUMBER
Build on what we know.

Follow the Steelers
on and off the field.

| 7 | 7 | 1st & 10 | Ball on 24 | 2nd Qtr | 5:26 |

5:26

ADVANCED
MUNICATIONS
SOLUTIONS

McDonald's

40

UPMC

Steelers.com

PARKER
39

goalpost

end zone

FOOTBALL

red zone

sideline

10 20 30 40 50 40 30 20 10
10 20 30 40 50 40 30 20 10

midfield

hash mark

red zone

goalpost

end zone

FOOTBALL

14

The Football Field

An NFL field is 100 yards long. At each end is an **end zone** that is another 10 yards deep. Short white **hash marks** on the field mark off every yard. Longer lines mark every five yards. Numbers on the field help fans know where the players are. Goalposts stand at the back of each end zone. On some plays, a team can kick the football through the goalposts to earn points. During the game, each team stands along one sideline of the field. Heinz Field is covered with real grass. Some indoor NFL stadiums use **artificial**, or fake, grass.

During a game, the two teams stand on the sidelines. They usually stand near midfield, waiting for their turns to play. Coaches walk on the sidelines, too, along with cheerleaders and photographers.

Big Days!

The Pittsburgh Steelers have had many great moments in their long history. Here are three of the greatest:

1975: The Steelers won their first Super Bowl! Their great defense held up. They beat the Minnesota Vikings 16–6.

1980: Pittsburgh became the first team to win four Super Bowls! They beat the Los Angeles Rams 31–19.

2009: The Steelers returned to the top of the NFL. They won their second Super Bowl in four years. It took an exciting, last-minute pass to beat the Arizona Cardinals 27–23.

What a catch! Santonio Holmes (10) came down with this catch in the end zone. It gave the Steelers a come-from-behind win in the Super Bowl!

17

Tough Days!

The Steelers can't win all their games. Some games or seasons don't turn out well. The players keep trying to play their best, though! Here are some painful memories from Steelers history:

1939-1941: A bad time for the team! In three seasons, they won only four games.

1943-1944: The nation was fighting in World War II. Many NFL players joined the military. The Steelers joined the Philadelphia Eagles and the Chicago Cardinals to form two wartime teams—the "Steagles" and the "Card-Pitt." In 1944, they didn't win any games!

1969: The Steelers won only one game—it was their worst season ever!

Here's action from the Steelers' tough 1940 season. Notice anything odd about the kicker? He's not wearing a helmet!

Meet the Fans

Pittsburgh fans love their team! Until the 1970s, they didn't have much to root for. But they stuck with the Steelers. They are famous for waving bright yellow towels. The "Terrible Towels" spin and spin above the fans' heads. They create a sea of yellow! Pittsburgh fans put up with cold weather and snow to watch their favorite team.

A radio announcer suggested that fans start waving yellow towels during games. It caught on, and today it's a big part of every Steelers game.

Heroes Then . . .

Most of the Steelers' past heroes played on their Super Bowl teams. Quarterback Terry Bradshaw won two Super Bowl Most Valuable Player awards. **Wide receivers** Lynn Swann and John Stallworth made dozens of amazing catches. Running back Franco Harris was super-hard to tackle. Defenders known as the "Steel Curtain" were hard to beat at the **line of scrimmage**! These tough players included **linebackers** Jack Ham and Jack Lambert, **defensive tackle** "Mean" Joe Greene, and **cornerback** Mel Blount.

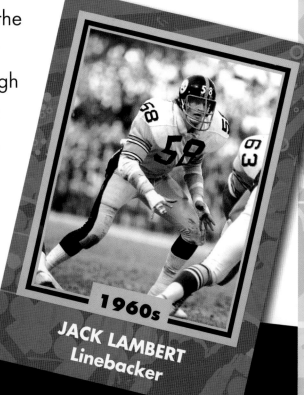

1960s

JACK LAMBERT
Linebacker

On the way to four Super Bowl wins, the Pittsburgh offense was led by Bradshaw (left). The defense was anchored by Jack Lambert.

Heroes Now . . .

The biggest hero for today's Steelers is "Big Ben." That's what fans call quarterback Ben Roethlisberger. He led them to a Super Bowl title as a **rookie** and has been a star ever since. Running back Willie Parker is fast and strong. Wide receiver Hines Ward has several team records. On defense, **safety** Troy Polamalu is famous for his long, wild hair. He's also one of the NFL's best at his position. Linebackers James Harrison and James Farrior are a powerful one-two team.

BEN ROETHLISBERGER
Quarterback

HINES WARD
Wide Receiver

TROY POLAMALU
Safety

25

Gearing Up

Pittsburgh Steelers players wear lots of gear to help keep them safe. They wear pads from head to toe. Check out this picture of Troy Polamalu and learn what NFL players wear.

The Football

NFL footballs are made of four panels of leather. White laces help the quarterback grip and throw the ball. Inside the football is a rubber bag that holds air.

Football Fact

NFL footballs don't have white lines around them. Only college teams use footballs with those lines.

helmet

facemask

shoulder pad

chest pad

NO thigh pad (ouch!)

knee pad

cleats

27

Sports Stats

Note: All numbers are through the 2008 season.

TOUCHDOWN MAKERS

These players have scored the most touchdowns for the Steelers.

PLAYER	TOUCHDOWNS
Franco Harris	100
Jerome Bettis	80

PASSING FANCY

Top Steelers quarterbacks

PLAYER	PASSING YARDS
Terry Bradshaw	27,989
Ben Roethlisberger	14,974

RUN FOR GLORY

Top Steelers running backs

PLAYER	RUSHING YARDS
Franco Harris	11,950
Jerome Bettis	10,571

Receivers

CATCH A STAR
Top Steelers receivers

PLAYER	CATCHES
Hines Ward	800
John Stallworth	537

TOP DEFENDERS
Steelers defensive records

Most **interceptions**: Mel Blount, 57
Most **sacks**: Jason Gildon, 77

Defenders

COACH
Most Coaching Wins

Chuck Noll, 209

Coach

Glossary

artificial fake, not real

cornerback a player who covers the other team's receivers and tries to keep them from making catches

defense players who are trying to keep the other team from scoring

defensive tackle a player who starts each play in the middle of the defensive line

end zone a 10-yard-deep area at each end of the field

hash marks short white lines that mark off each yard on the football field

interceptions catches made by defensive players

linebackers defensive players who begin each play standing behind the main defensive line

line of scrimmage the place where the two teams face off when a play starts

offense players who have the ball and are trying to score

quarterback the key offensive player who starts each play and passes or hands off to a teammate

receivers offensive players who catch forward passes

rivals teams that play each other often and have an ongoing competition

rookie a new player

running back an offensive player who runs with the football and catches passes

sacks tackles of a quarterback behind the line of scrimmage

safety a defensive player who lines up farthest from the football and keeps receivers from making catches

Super Bowl the NFL's yearly championship game

touchdowns six-point scores made by carrying or catching the ball in the end zone

wide receivers offensive players who start each play to one side of the team and run to catch the ball

Find Out More

BOOKS

Buckley, James Jr. *The Scholastic Ultimate Book of Football*. New York: Scholastic, 2009.

Madden, John, and Bill Gutman. *Heroes of Football*. New York: Dutton, 2006.

Polzer, Tim. *Play Football! A Guide for Young Players from the National Football League*. New York: DK Publishing, 2002.

Sandler, Michael. *Ben Roethlisberger: Football Heroes Making a Difference*. New York: Bearport Publishing, 2009.

Stewart, Mark, and Jason Akins. *The Pittsburgh Steelers*. Chicago: Norwood House Press, 2006.

WEB SITE

Visit our Web site for lots of links about the Pittsburgh Steelers and other NFL football teams:

childsworld.com/links

Note to Parents, Teachers, and Librarians: We routinely verify our Web links to make sure they are safe, active sites—so encourage your readers to check them out!

Index

About the Author

K. C. Kelley is a huge football fan! He has written dozens of books on football and other sports for young readers. K. C. used to work for NFL Publishing and has covered several Super Bowls.